THE GOLEM

Man of Earth

A Play in Two Acts

by
Howard Rubenstein

based on historical events,
a medieval Jewish legend, kabbalah,
and the Yiddish dramatic poem
by H. Leivick

Granite Hills Press™

THE GOLEM, MAN OF EARTH
A Play in Two Acts
by Howard Rubenstein
based on historical events, a medieval Jewish legend,
kabbalah, and the Yiddish dramatic poem by H. Leivick.

Published 2007 by Granite Hills Press™
SAN 298-072X
Cover by Chuck Conners, cyberwatercolor based on a
photograph by Judith S. Rubenstein

Cataloging in Publication
Rubenstein, Howard S., 1931–
    The golem, man of earth : a play in two acts / by Howard
    Rubenstein ; based on historical events, a medieval Jewish
    legend, kabbalah, and the Yiddish dramatic poem by H.
    Leivick.
    p. cm.
    LCCN: 2007903452
    ISBN-13: 978-1-929468-12-6
    ISBN-10: 1-929468-12-1
    1. Blood libel--Drama. 2. Pogroms--Drama. 3. Golem--
    Drama. 4. Religious intolerance--Drama. 5. Christian
    persecution of the Jews--Drama.
I. Halper, Leivick (H. Leivick), 1888–1962.
II. Title.

Printed in the United States of America

To "liberty and justice for all"

CONTENTS

ACKNOWLEDGMENTS

The Golem, Man of Earth is based on the Yiddish work *The Golem, A Dramatic Poem in Eight Scenes* (1921) by H. Leivick (the pen name of Leivick Halper, 1888–1962) as translated into English by Joseph C. Landis (1966) and Joachim Neugroschel (2006). The latter translation was used principally to confirm parts of the earlier one.

An experimental version of *The Golem, Man of Earth* was produced by 6th@Penn Theatre, San Diego, and had its first performance on October 15, 2006. It was directed by Zoe Paulin and Dale Morris, with the following cast: S. Michael Barron (Golem), Mikel Taxer (Maharal), Renée Gandola (Pearl/Redhead), Bonnie Alexander (Eva/Blonde), James Steinberg (Bashevi/Blind Man), Michael Tower (Old Priest/Old Wanderer), Alberto Alvarado (Young Priest/Young Wanderer), and Terence J. Burke (Yankl).

I thank the directors and the cast for asking many questions and making many suggestions that clarified and helped develop the final script, which is this published version. I thank Ingar Quist for editing drafts of the book. As always, I thank my wife, Judy, for her many questions and suggestions, for editing all drafts, and especially for her constant and loving support.

Howard Rubenstein
San Diego
June 25, 2007

INTRODUCTION

A golem is a man-made man created out of earth by a righteous person through the magic of kabbalistic incantation. The incantation requires the uttering of certain Hebrew letters, parts of kabbalistic literature (especially sections in the *Book of Creation*, a Jewish medieval mystical work), and finally the ineffable name of God. The word *golem* appears in the Bible only once, in Psalm 139:16, where it means "formless."

The legend of the golem originated among European Jews in the early Middle Ages. At that time, antisemitism was particularly virulent because the church fostered one of the most malignant of slanders and libels, namely, that the Jews murdered a gentile child during the Easter season to obtain Christian blood for their Passover festival. That lie, called by historians the "blood libel," incited the Christian community to carry out massacres of Jews known as pogroms. The purpose of the golem was to protect the Jews against these pogroms.

Even today in a free and civilized society where pogroms do not occur, the blood libel continues to be disturbing. Many Christians do not want to remember that some of them ever behaved so maliciously, and many Jews do not wish to remind them, lest talking about the libel might revive its malignant consequences. Unfortunately, Christian antisemitism has deep roots and long runners. Hitler spread the libel in his war against the Jews, and radical Islam, even though the libel concerns the murder of Christians, spreads it today. Civilization cannot advance without acknowledging its harmful past so that it will not repeat it.

In the twentieth century, the legend of the golem became the subject of a famous Yiddish dramatic poem by H. Leivick. His work, translated into English, was the principal basis for my play (see acknowledgments). I adapted and reworked it, inserted relevant kabbalah, and added material of my own to make a play accessible to a general audience.

According to most versions of the legend, the golem was stupid, mute, and devoid of feelings. But in my version, as in Leivick's, the creature turns out to be highly intelligent and articulate and to have such profound depths of human feelings that he is incapable of successfully carrying out his mission.

The Golem, Man of Earth is more than a Jewish play. It comes with grave warnings that humanity cannot depend on the magical and the supernatural for protection, and that force, terror, and violence, however justifiable, cannot successfully resolve human problems. The play is also a metaphor for man's relationship to God and man's relationship to man. Finally, it is about the never-ending struggle for human dignity and human rights, and ultimately human survival.

Howard Rubenstein

THE GOLEM

Man of Earth

CHARACTERS

GOLEM. A legendary man-made man of earth (including his disembodied voice and spirit), ageless.

MAHARAL. A famous rabbi of sixteenth-century Prague, middle-aged. Maharal is a Hebrew acronym: MA-HA-RA-L, which means "Our Teacher, The Rabbi Loew" (MA-reinu [Our teacher] HA-RAv [The Rabbi] L [Loew]).

PEARL. The Maharal's wife, middle-aged.

EVA. Their granddaughter, adolescent.

BASHEVI. The father of the Maharal's murdered son-in-law, middle-aged.

OLD PRIEST.

YOUNG PRIEST.

The Homeless:

YANKL. A crazy man, self-appointed leader of the homeless.

REDHEAD.

BLIND MAN. With cane for the blind.

BLONDE.

OLD WANDERER. Possibly Elijah the Prophet.

YOUNG WANDERER. Possibly the Messiah.

2

SCENES

Time: Sixteenth century.
Place: Prague.

ACT I

Scene 1   A spring evening, the first day of
            Passover, with a low full moon.
            Just outside the Jewish quarter. The
            sky is orange and black because the
            Jewish quarter is in flames.

Scene 2   Two and a half years later. A
            deserted place on the banks of the
            Moldau River. A clear autumn
            night shortly before dawn. The sky
            is black and filled with stars.

Scene 3   Later that morning. The Maharal's
            living room in his home in the
            Jewish quarter.

Scene 4   That afternoon. The Maharal's
            study in his home.

Scene 5   That night. The castle tower in the
            Jewish quarter.

4

ACT II

ACT I

Scene 1

Prague, sixteenth century. A spring evening, the first day of Passover, with a low full moon. Just outside the Jewish quarter. The sky is orange and black because the Jewish quarter is in flames. After a moment the OLD PRIEST *runs in carrying a burning torch and speaks to the audience.*

OLD PRIEST. (*Shouting.*) Quiet, everyone! Quiet! (*When all are quiet, in a normal voice.*) As you know, this is Holy Week. This coming Friday is Good Friday. Sunday is Easter. I expect to see you all at mass on Sunday.

    The Passover of the Jews has just begun. I don't have to tell you that the Jews killed Christ our God at Passover. Recently these wretched people have resorted to killing our children to obtain blood for their Passover celebration. They love to eat their unholy unleavened bread baked with the blood of Christian children.

We have already set fire to many Jewish homes, (*Pointing.*) as you can see. I myself have set fire to quite a few. If you've not done so already, it's not too late. And while you're at it, kill a Jew for Christ! Kill a Jew for this year's murdered Christian child! (*Pause.*) I look forward to seeing you all at church on Sunday. (*He runs off.*)

(*Fade-out.*)

Scene 2

Two and a half years later. A deserted place on the banks of the Moldau River. A clear autumn night shortly before dawn. The sky is black and filled with stars. The MAHARAL is standing over a mound of earth shaped in the form of a giant man lying supine. The mound is covered with a thin blanket of brown burlap so that the human form is somewhat obscured to show that the creature is not yet fully formed.

MAHARAL. It's been two and a half years since the last pogrom in Prague. That was incited by the lie that we kill Christian children to get blood for our Passover feast. They say this even when they know we are forbidden by the Torah to eat blood, and when they know

"Thou shalt not murder" is one of the Ten Commandments. They tell these lies to justify murdering us.

(*The* MAHARAL *kneels and with both hands gently molds the face of the mound and applies the finishing touches.*)

There! I'm finished! (*Standing.*)

Through the magic power
of Hebrew letters, words, and speech,
I'll imbue my image with life.
I create a golem, a man-made man of earth,
to be the Jews' protector
against murders, massacres, and pogroms.
(*Pause.*)
Here, on the banks of the River Moldau,
on the outskirts of the city of Prague,
shortly before dawn,
cut off from every living thing,
I chant the incantation of creation.

(*Lifting his arms over the mound and chanting Hebrew words of magic.*)

   SAY-fair YUH-tsee-rah,
   Seh-fee-ROTE bel-lee MAH.
   Oh-tee-YOTE YEH-sod.

   (*A moaning wind followed by howling wolves and barking dogs.*)

In the *Book of Creation*
Kabbalah teaches about emanation:
"One spirit comes from another."
"Their end is in their beginning,
and their beginning is in their end."

(*Chanting Hebrew letters possessing magic.*)

Alef, mem, shin!

(*Dancing clockwise three times around the mound, then three times counterclockwise. Then lifting his arms over the mound and chanting Hebrew words of magic.*)

SAY-fair YUH-tsee-rah,
Seh-fee-ROTE bel-lee MAH.
Oh-tee-YOTE YEH-sod.

(*The sound of flapping wings. Frightened, the MAHARAL covers his ears with his hands.*)

I hear the rush of wings.

(*Brushing his hands wildly before his eyes.*)

Something just flew before my eyes!

(*Brushing his brow.*)

What brushed against my brow?

> (*Sound of loud screeching birds
> followed by silence. He gazes about
> bewildered.*)

And yet there's nothing here,
nothing but silence.
The river flows. The city sleeps.
Soon the stars will go out one by one,
and the eastern sky will glow
with the light of the newborn day.

> (*Suddenly terrified by something he sees on the
> river.*)

Who walks upon the surface of the river?
Who approaches, yet comes no nearer?
Who departs, yet goes not afar?
Who are you, Dark Presence
that chills my heart like an icy wind?
GOLEM. (*Voice of Spirit.*)
    You do not know?
MAHARAL. Your voice is like the blast
    that blows in a cave
    without entrance or exit.
    Who are you? Speak!
GOLEM. I am the spirit of the golem.
    I come to warn you:
    Create me not!
MAHARAL. Do not interfere, Spirit!

GOLEM. Heed my warning:
    Create me not!
MAHARAL. (*Turning to heaven.*)
    O God, help me in this gravest hour!
GOLEM. Listen to me!
    How good it is to lie lifeless and calm
    among the sand and clay and stones of earth
    for all eternity!
    Once created,
    whatever I touch
    may gush forth blood
    or disintegrate into dust.
MAHARAL. I was sent by God to create a man!
GOLEM. Were you really?
MAHARAL. Who are you to question me?
    I tell you that I know
    God wants me to create a man,
    and with the dawn
    to make the breath of life
    enter him.
GOLEM. For the last time: Create me not!
MAHARAL. Your wishes and desires
    count for naught.
    Your days and nights
    and all your deeds
    have been decreed
    by a power greater than you or me.
    You are created for more than life.
    You are meant to do great works and wonders.
    Until that time
    a woodcutter you shall be.

GOLEM. A woodcutter? No. A golem,
    a man-made man of earth.
MAHARAL. The people's protector!
    A man of might!
    Champion of the Jews!
    Their defender! (*Pause.*)
    Their savior!
GOLEM. Their savior?
    No. Their slave!
    To obey your commands.
MAHARAL. A living human being! A man!
GOLEM. (*Sardonically.*) A man.
    The night departs,
    the day approaches.
    Only one moment more
    to be what I've always been,
    lifeless clay and earth.
MAHARAL. (*To heaven.*)
    O Creator of the universe,
    I'm unworthy in your eyes.
    Audacious and proud,
    too eager to do what no one should do,
    to see what no one has seen.
    I am terrified! (*Pause.*)
    And yet, I cannot overcome temptation.
    My pride and ambition
    conquer all my fear. (*Pause.*)
    I tell myself that what I do
    I do out of love for you—
    to become one with you!
    (*Examining the mound.*)
    I create a man of might!

Soon he'll walk,
but what will be his ways? (*Pause.*)
Evil times of old,
evil times yet to be.
Tyrants tell lies
to slaughter the innocent. (*Pause.*)
O God! What am I?
Like my creation, a lump of clay.
And yet, all that I see will be!
This golem shall our protector be. (*Pause.*)
I lock forever in my heart
the secret I alone do know.
No one will ever hear it from me.
Never! Forever!

> (*The sky turns the rose and violet of
> early dawn. He turns to heaven.*)

Dawn is breaking. (*Pause.*)

(*Chanting the Hebrew letters of supreme magic
that form the ineffable name of God.*)

> *Yud, hay, vuv*!

> (*The mound of earth turns red.*)

O sacred and secret Name of God
that seals every act of creation!

(*Covering his eyes and mouth and muttering
"Jehovah," which in English may stand for the*

ineffable name. Spreading his arms over the mound.)

Spirit of the golem,
enter your home!
(*Emphatically.*) Enter now!

> (*Sound of rushing wind. The mound turns from red to black with a sizzling sound and emanates white vapor, as if someone had plunged a red-hot piece of iron into cold water. The* MAHARAL *stands back in astonishment. Then, after a moment, he recites* Genesis 2:7.)

"Then the Lord God formed man
of dust from the ground
and breathed into his nostrils
the breath of life;
and man became a living being."

(*Staring at the mound, then speaking in great excitement.*)

The mound of earth is beginning to stir!
Its arms and legs are moving!
It's happening! The lump of clay is alive!
This is the dawning of a day of miracles!

> (*The* GOLEM *very slowly stands. The burlap blanket that covered the*

mound and kept its form somewhat
obscured slips off the body, and the
well-defined silhouette of a naked
giant can be seen stretching his
arms against the late dawn's yellow
sky.)

(*Fade-out.*)

Scene 3

Later that morning. The Maharal's living room in
his home in the Jewish quarter. At the door, the
MAHARAL *has crossed the threshold into the*
house. The GOLEM, *wearing a short-sleeved shirt,*
full-length trousers, and shoes, stands at the
threshold. He does not enter because he is too tall
and does not know enough to stoop.

MAHARAL. (*Kindly.*) Stoop!
    Bend your neck and lower your head!
    You are tall.
    When one is tall
    and wishes to come through a door that's low,
    one must stoop.
    Watch me! Like this!

        (*The   MAHARAL   demonstrates:*
        He exits, turns, stoops, and reenters.

The GOLEM *imitates and enters but does not straighten up.*)

Now straighten up!

(*The* GOLEM *does so.*)

That's right.

(*The* GOLEM *stares around the room.*)

This is my home.
As we walked here,
you saw the sky above,
the sun rising in the east.
You've seen people on the streets.
In this neighborhood,
you've seen Jews in the courtyards. (*Pause.*)
There's no need to remain silent.
I know you can speak.
Your spirit spoke to me by the river
before it entered your body.
Speak. I command you to speak.
Joseph is your name.
GOLEM. (*Marvels.*) *Joseph.*
MAHARAL. Yes! Joseph! You are a man.
GOLEM. (*Marvels.*) A *man.*
MAHARAL. Yes, a man. You are alive.
GOLEM. (*Marvels.*) *Alive.*
MAHARAL. Yes.
    Now, do you remember your name?

(*The* GOLEM *is silent.*)

Have you forgotten?
I will remind you.
Your name is Joseph.
Remember it!
GOLEM. Joseph.
MAHARAL. Yes. (*Pause.*) What is your name?
GOLEM. Joseph. My name is Joseph.
MAHARAL. Very good, Joseph.
My name is Judah Loew, Rabbi Judah Loew,
but people call me the Maharal.
Can you say "Maharal"?
GOLEM. Maharal.
MAHARAL. Good, very good.

    (*Suddenly the* GOLEM *strides
about the room. He crashes into a
wall and begins to push on it.*)

Stop! You must not do that! Besides,
you will awaken everyone in the house!
GOLEM. I want to leave this place! (*Pounding
on the wall.*)
MAHARAL. I tell you, stop!
Don't pound on walls!
GOLEM. (*Stopping.*) I want to leave this place!
MAHARAL. You must do whatever I command!
GOLEM. (*Sitting on the floor like a child.*)
I will obey you,
but still I want to leave this place.

MAHARAL. You will do as I say.
>You will get used to things.
>Be patient.
>Now, tell me, do you remember your name?
GOLEM. My name is Joseph—
>and I want to leave this place!
>Joseph wants to leave!
MAHARAL. Joseph, get off the floor
>and sit on a bench.
>One does not sit on the floor.
>One sits on a bench or in a chair.

>(*The* GOLEM *sits on a bench.*)

>Good! I think you must be tired.
>You've already learned much and seen much.
>No wonder you're tired.
>Soon you'll sleep.
>I want you to know
>you are welcome in my house.
GOLEM. (*Showing he understands.*)
>I am welcome.
MAHARAL. Yes. Welcome.
>I found you on the outskirts of town
>on the banks of the river.
>You were asleep.
GOLEM. I don't remember. (*Suddenly agitated, jumping up and walking rapidly about the room.*)
MAHARAL. Joseph, what's the matter?
GOLEM. I want to leave! I want to go right now!
>I'm afraid to stay.

MAHARAL. You have nothing to fear.
GOLEM. I want to go!
    Don't try to stop me!
    You are so old,
    and you are so little!
MAHARAL. Have you forgotten who I am?
GOLEM. Who *are* you?
MAHARAL. I am your master.
    You are my servant.
    You are under my command.
GOLEM. What must I do?
MAHARAL. Nothing for now.
    Your moment has not yet come. (*Pause.*)
    Do you want to live with me?
GOLEM. No!
MAHARAL. Well, you cannot go!
    You are a stranger in town.
    Here, in my house,
    you will feel at home.
GOLEM. I must go!
    What is there for me here?
    I want to run away,
    and yet you tell me I must stay.
    Let me go!
    How easy it would be
    to seize you by the neck! (*Shouting.*)
    I want to strike my fist down hard
    upon your head!
    And yet I cannot.
    I want to smash and destroy!
    I want to twist my own head
    off my shoulders!

(*Hurling himself against the wall, pounding it with his fists, rattling the wall.*)

MAHARAL. Stop that! Stop!

(*He gently places a hand on the GOLEM's shoulder, calming him.*)

That's better. Your shoulders are trembling.
Sit down! You have nothing to fear.

(*The GOLEM sits at a small table. The MAHARAL places a hand on the GOLEM's head.   After a moment, the MAHARAL removes his hand.*)

There! I have blessed you,
and you are a blessing.
You don't know yet what you are, who you are.
For now, know that you are welcome.
Let that be sufficient to keep you calm.

(*Sound of footsteps.*)

Someone's coming.
You've awakened everyone
with your pounding and shouting.
Say nothing to anyone
except that you are a stranger
from a faraway land
and that you are a guest in my house.

Let that be your reply to everyone:
You are a stranger and a guest.
GOLEM. (*Showing he understands.*)
I am a stranger and a guest.
MAHARAL. Yes.

>(PEARL, *the Maharal's wife, and*
>EVA, *their granddaughter, wearing*
>*nightgowns, enter frightened.*)

PEARL. Maharal, what's the matter?
What was all that noise?
What shook the house so?
MAHARAL. You must have had a bad dream.
PEARL. Then Eva and I both
had the same bad dream.
And in our dream,
we were thrown from our beds!
(*She notices the* GOLEM, *who cannot take his*
eyes off EVA.)
Who is that sitting there?
EVA. How strange he looks!
MAHARAL. He is a stranger and a guest.
This morning
when I went to bathe in the river,
I saw him lying on the ground,
exhausted from his travels.
And so I invited him home.
PEARL. I don't think he's Jewish.
He doesn't look Jewish to me.
And he makes me uncomfortable.
MAHARAL. No need to fear him.

EVA. See how he stares!
　　He doesn't take his eyes off me.
　　What does he want, Grampa? Ask him!
MAHARAL. He doesn't like to answer questions.
EVA. He has sad eyes.
PEARL. I feel sorry for him, and yet—
　　he makes me uncomfortable.
　　Stranger, what is your name?
GOLEM. Joseph. (*Grinning, proud of what he is
　　about to say, looking at the* MAHARAL *for
　　approval.*)
　　I am a stranger and a guest.

> (*The* MAHARAL *smiles with
> approval. The* GOLEM *stands and
> looks with wonder at* EVA.)

　　Maharal, *who is she*?
EVA. Oh, Gramma, let's leave.
　　He frightens me.
PEARL. Doesn't he have any sense,
　　to stare at her so?
GOLEM. Who is she, Maharal?
MAHARAL. She is my granddaughter.
　　I don't want you to stare at her.
　　I don't want you to look at her.
　　And don't speak to her either.
GOLEM. She has long hair.
　　I like the way
　　it falls down behind her shoulders.
　　It is pretty. She is pretty.
EVA. Let's go. I'm afraid of him.

PEARL. It is disgraceful for a man
to say such things.
MAHARAL. He doesn't know what he's saying.
PEARL. He doesn't? *Really*?
I don't think *you* know what you're saying.
GOLEM. Food! I want food!
MAHARAL. Yes, of course.
He's had no breakfast.
Bring him some food.

(PEARL *and* EVA *retreat into the
house*.)

GOLEM. Where did she go?
MAHARAL. To get you some food, some
breakfast.
GOLEM. I felt so good whenever she looked at me.
MAHARAL. Don't talk about her anymore.
GOLEM. I want to take her by the hand. May I
do that?
MAHARAL. No, you may not! You may not
even look at her! Be silent when she is near.
GOLEM. Is there no one I can speak to?
MAHARAL. You can speak to me. And if people
ask you questions, you may answer them. But
try to stay as far away from people as you can.
In that way, they won't speak to you. That is
the road to happiness.
GOLEM. Silence and avoiding people bring
happiness? (*Glumly sitting down at the table,
turning his head away*.) It has suddenly grown
very dark. I'm afraid.

MAHARAL. You're hungry. After you've eaten, you'll feel better.

> (PEARL *and* EVA *return.* EVA, *carrying a glass of milk and a roll in a small bread basket, sets down the food before the* GOLEM. *He eats and drinks voraciously.*)

PEARL. He eats bread without first blessing it. He's not a Jew. And look how he gulps down the milk!

MAHARAL. He's hungry. (*Pause.*) Well, should I invite him to stay or not?

PEARL. To stay? With us?

MAHARAL. Of course, with us! With whom else should he stay? I need a man to split wood.

PEARL. Eva is afraid of him. Who is he?

MAHARAL. He's an honest and lonely man. And he will cut our wood.

PEARL. Well, if you say so.

MAHARAL. Are you afraid of him, too?

PEARL. Yes.

MAHARAL. No need. God has blessed us by placing him in our path.

PEARL. God has *blessed* us? What do you mean?

MAHARAL. I've long needed a man to cut wood, a man of strength like him. And now we have one.

PEARL. I guess you know what you're doing. (*To the* GOLEM.) Have you had enough to eat? Do you want some more?

(*The* GOLEM *shakes his head.*)

EVA. Is he going to remain here for long?
MAHARAL. I don't know yet.
EVA. Look! His eyes are still glued to me.
PEARL. Let's go!

(PEARL *and* EVA, *picking up the empty glass and bread basket, retreat into the house.*)

GOLEM. (*Yawns.*) Maharal, my eyes feel heavy.
MAHARAL. That means you're sleepy. Soon you'll fall asleep. And when you awaken, you'll be refreshed, and the world will seem different.

(*The* GOLEM *nods off at the table. Moments later he awakens with a start.*)

GOLEM. I want to go! I must go! (*Standing and walking toward the door to the outside.*) Something tells me to go.

(*The* MAHARAL *blocks him with his hand.*)

MAHARAL. No, you may not go! Sit!
GOLEM. (*Returning to his chair and sitting.*) Where's Eva?
MAHARAL. (*Angrily.*) Eva? Didn't I tell you to forget her?

GOLEM. Why are you angry, Maharal?
MAHARAL. I'm not angry.
 You're only imagining it.
 But never mention Eva again!

  (*The* GOLEM *grows glum.*)

 Do you understand?
GOLEM. I heard you, Maharal. I will obey you.
 Now my eyes are very heavy. (*Yawning, then
 falling asleep sitting up, breathing deeply.*)
MAHARAL.   He's asleep!   (*Staring at him.*)
 Newly created, and yet so much feeling.
 Is this the man I created?
 Is this our *protector*?
 So big his hands!
 So broad his shoulders!
 So big his arms—and legs!
 So great his feelings! Can this be?

  (PEARL *enters.*)

PEARL. Why is it so quiet in here?
MAHARAL. (*Whispering.*) Shh! He's asleep. He
 needs to sleep.
PEARL. So do you. Come to bed.

  (*Fade-out.*)

Scene 4

That afternoon. The Maharal's study in his home. The MAHARAL *is asleep in a chair, snoring, holding an open book.*

MAHARAL. (*In his sleep, indistinctly.*) Golem! Blood! Blood! Fire! Fire! (*Pause.*) Joseph!
EVA. (*Running in.*) Grampa, wake up!
MAHARAL. (*Waking startled.*) What! What is it?
EVA. You cried out in your sleep.
MAHARAL. I must have been dreaming.
EVA. You were shouting, "Blood! Fire!"
MAHARAL. It's nothing. It was just a dream. I'm all right. You can go.

> (EVA *exits. The* MAHARAL *promptly nods off again. After a while, the* GOLEM *appears in the doorway, dangling an ax, watching the* MAHARAL. *Then he enters the room, staring at the* MAHARAL *and imitating his snoring and head motions. Suddenly the* MAHARAL *awakens with a start. To the* GOLEM.)

How did you get in here?

GOLEM. I walked through the door—just as you taught me. I saw you sitting and sleeping.

MAHARAL. What made you come?

GOLEM. You called me. You shouted, "Joseph!"

MAHARAL. (*Puzzled.*) I called you? Go back to work. Go back to splitting wood. That's your job. (*Pause.*) Now pay attention. You must never bring your ax indoors. It belongs in your hands when you're cutting wood, and it belongs in the woodshed when you're not. Have you split all the wood for today?

GOLEM. They don't let me do my work.

MAHARAL. Who doesn't let you do your work?

GOLEM. *They* don't. They make fun of me.

MAHARAL. Who makes fun of you?

GOLEM. The boys—and the men, too. They stand around and stare at me. They ask me my name. And so I tell them. And then they ask me where I'm from. And I don't know how to answer them.

MAHARAL. Don't answer them at all. You don't have to answer them.

GOLEM. I don't? But if I'm quiet, that annoys them. (*Pause.*) Maharal, where *do* I come from?

MAHARAL. Don't ask! You must not ask!

GOLEM. So I can't answer them, even if I want to.

MAHARAL. They will not harm you.

GOLEM. I hate them!

MAHARAL. You *hate* them? You must learn to live peaceably with everyone.

GOLEM. Do you live peaceably with everyone? Do the Jews live peaceably with the non-Jews?

MAHARAL. What made you ask such a question?

GOLEM. Am I a Jew, Maharal?

If you're a Jew, I want to be one, too.

MAHARAL. No, you're not a Jew—not yet.
You're not ready. You have to study first. For
now you must cut wood.

GOLEM. (*Mocking.*) I must cut wood—and not
look at anyone and not talk to anyone!
(*Pause.*) They all stare at me, Maharal.

MAHARAL. Don't worry about it, and don't be
afraid. Go back to work. I'll go out and talk to
them and tell them to leave you alone.

GOLEM. I don't think that'll do any good.
They're not afraid of you, Maharal. I know
that. I've said to them many times, "The
Maharal will come out and scold you." And
whenever I say that, they only laugh.

MAHARAL. Go back to work.

GOLEM. One laughed so hard—and would not
stop!—I was ready to let him have it with my
ax.

MAHARAL. What are you saying?

GOLEM. Oh, Maharal, drive them away. Why do
they enjoy tormenting me so? Why do you
teach me not to raise an ax to them?

MAHARAL. You must not harm them. An ax is
only for cutting wood.

GOLEM. I hate them! I hate them all! I hate
you, too!

MAHARAL. *Me*, too?

GOLEM. Yes, you, too!

I can always hear your voice saying,

"Where are you?"
And I strike the ax into the wood and say,
"Here I am."
And all the people begin to laugh and say,
"Here I am. Here I am."
And then they laugh louder and say,
"*Hee-NAY-nee.*"

MAHARAL. (*Smiling.*) That's what Abraham said to God to show his devotion to him, to show he was always ready to obey his commands. *Hee-NAY-nee* is Hebrew for "Here I am."

GOLEM. So! I am like Abraham, and you are like God?

MAHARAL. No.

GOLEM. Then why do they laugh?

MAHARAL. They're making a joke. But you're right. It's not funny. Go back to work, and don't listen to them.

GOLEM. Maharal, the first time I straightened up from splitting logs and saw so many faces and eyes looking at me, I thought they liked me and enjoyed watching me work. But soon I saw I was mistaken. They started calling me names and laughing. I thought I heard your laughter, too.

MAHARAL. *Mine?*

GOLEM. Yes. I thought you were laughing and shouting in contempt, "Golem!" "Golem!" That's why I quit working and came to see you just now, to see whether it was so.

MAHARAL. Do you feel better now that we've talked?

GOLEM. I always feel good when I'm with you.

MAHARAL. You see me many times during the day. And whenever you need me, you can always come and speak to me, just as you've done now.

GOLEM. They come to watch me chop wood. How come you don't? I want you to watch me chop wood! Don't you want to?

MAHARAL. (*Reflecting.*) He thinks like a little boy!

GOLEM. Another thing. Where do I sleep? In the woodshed, all by myself?

MAHARAL. Not if you don't want to. You can sleep in the tower of the old castle. The homeless Jews sleep there. You'll have lots of company, and you'll not miss me.

GOLEM. Why won't you sleep there?

MAHARAL. Well, I have my family here—my wife and my granddaughter. And then there's the congregation, the Jews that come to the shul—the synagogue—the big building next door. They, too, need me here. (*Pause.*) At the castle, you'll make friends who'll be like family. (*Pause.*) I can't always be with you. You came here to do your work. So there are times when you'll be all alone. And when you're finished working, you can go to the castle tower and sleep there. (*Pause.*) Go back to work now. I'll call you if I need you.

(*The* GOLEM *exits, ax in hand.
The ax does not appear again until
the final scene.*)

(*To himself.*) Great dangers threaten.
And yet,
he is so helpless, this golem.
Helpless himself,
how is he ever going to help us?
Besides,
he has giant passions in his giant body.
I am afraid.

BASHEVI. (*Entering.*) Good evening, Maharal.

MAHARAL. Hello, Bashevi! I didn't see you come in. Sit down.

BASHEVI. (*Sitting.*) I thought it might be a good idea to come and speak with the Maharal.

MAHARAL. What's troubling you, Bashevi?

BASHEVI. The woodcutter in the courtyard. He's enough to scare a person half to death.

MAHARAL. There's nothing to fear. A woodcutter doing his work, nothing more.

BASHEVI. I don't think this man has made any friends. When I first saw him, I must admit, I couldn't help but stare. That giant with an ax! Who is he, Maharal? Do you know?

MAHARAL. Of course, I know! He's a stranger from far away.

BASHEVI. So we've nothing to fear, because you know him.

MAHARAL. There's no cause for fear, Bashevi. God is our Father.

BASHEVI. Those are comforting words, Maharal.
But how can we not be afraid? We are sinful,
and the times are bad. God punishes the wicked
for their sins.

MAHARAL. Perhaps we are magnifying the
danger?

BASHEVI. Perhaps. But what if the opposite is
true? What if the danger exceeds our fears?

It was only two years ago at Passover when
the mob came in the night with burning torches
and murdered Isaac, my son—your son-in-law,
Maharal—and murdered Rebecca, Isaac's wife
—your daughter, Maharal. Eva escaped only
because she was away from home that night,
spending it with you and Pearl. (*Pause*.)

Tell me, Maharal, what exactly do they
want of us?

MAHARAL. What do they want of us? More
than we can give. We wish them no harm, but
they constantly want to harm us. How can we
defend ourselves when we are so few and they
are so many? It's a paradox, not wishing them
harm, while wishing to protect ourselves.
(*Pause*.)

We have touched the world and everything
in it, and the world and everything in it is
forever better for our touch. Still, they want
something more. What is it they want? I'll
tell you what they want—to rid the world of us.

BASHEVI. I don't sleep well at night, Maharal. I
feel anguish.

MAHARAL. You're not alone. Who doesn't feel
anguish? It's part of life, Bashevi, not only for
us but for them, too. Perhaps we feel it more.
(*Pause.*)
     And yet, what if you or I were to raise a
hand to protect ourselves? What do you think
would happen?

BASHEVI. Catastrophe! Catastrophe for us all!

MAHARAL. Yes! But what if it wasn't you or I
who raised a hand? What if it was the
woodcutter in the courtyard? What then?
(*Stopping abruptly, frightened.*)

BASHEVI. What's the matter, Maharal? What's
wrong?

MAHARAL. A noise! Didn't you hear it?

BASHEVI. No. I heard nothing.

MAHARAL. (*Looking out the window, then
opening the door and looking outside.*) I must
have imagined it. There's no one in the
courtyard. Everything's quiet.

BASHEVI. What am I to say, Maharal, now that I
see how fearful you are?

MAHARAL. What are you to say? Nothing!

BASHEVI. I wanted to hear comforting words,
Maharal.

MAHARAL. Comforting words? Here are
comforting words: All fears are needless.

BASHEVI. *Needless*?

MAHARAL. Yes, without foundation. Rest
assured, Bashevi, you can sleep well at night.
All the Jews of Prague can sleep well. No one
should ever go without sleep, and no one should

ever grow so old as not to believe in miracles.
Yes, there still are miracles, Bashevi, and, yes,
you can sleep well at night. You have my word
on it. You may go now, Bashevi.

(BASHEVI, *perplexed and shaking
his head, leaves. After a moment,*
YANKL *rushes in.*)

Yankl! Sit down!

YANKL. No, Maharal. I have no time to sit.
Elijah the Prophet is coming in his chariot of
fire and bringing with him the Messiah.

MAHARAL. I'm glad to hear it, Yankl. Now,
what's upsetting you? Something at the castle
tower?

YANKL. No, I'm still in charge there. And I can
report to you, Maharal, that all sorrows at the
tower remain the same.

MAHARAL. But you are upset, Yankl. Is it
something here in the courtyard?

YANKL. Well, the woodcutter in the courtyard is
terrifying everyone, but not me. Yankl has no
fear of a giant swinging an ax.

MAHARAL. Well, then, Yankl, what *is* upsetting
you?

YANKL. I want to know who's in charge! Tell
me who's in charge here, the Maharal or the
priest?

MAHARAL. Why do you ask?

YANKL. Did you know that the priest just came
by to check out the castle tower? Did you

know that, Maharal? That's why I left the
tower and came to see you.

MAHARAL. I knew.

YANKL. You knew? Then you know
he wants to drive me out
along with all the other homeless Jews
living in the castle tower.
But who's in charge here—
you, Maharal—
Our Teacher, the Rabbi Loew—
or me, Yankl—
Lord of the castle ruins?
Or could it be the woodcutter
in the courtyard?
(*Pause.*) Mmm? Maharal? (*Pause.*)
Well, it doesn't really matter.
For Elijah is coming in his chariot of fire
bringing the Messiah.
And I must get ready to receive them!
And so, good-bye, Maharal.

MAHARAL. Good-bye, Yankl.

> (YANKL *runs out. After a
> moment,* PEARL *and* EVA *enter
> from the outside, agitated.*)

MAHARAL. What's the matter? What happened?

PEARL. I'm too ashamed to speak of it.

MAHARAL. Tell me! What happened?

PEARL. The woodcutter—

MAHARAL. What has he done?

PEARL. He frightened Eva nearly to death!

MAHARAL. What did he do?

PEARL. He grabbed her and kissed her!

MAHARAL. Oh, my God! Oh, God in heaven!
     What's he doing now?

PEARL. He's standing perfectly still outside the
     front door, looking like a statue, turned to
     stone.

EVA. Grampa, make him go away!

MAHARAL. Don't worry! Go to your rooms!
     I'll take care of it!

> (PEARL *and* EVA *retreat into the
> house.*)

> (*Calling.*) Joseph.
> (*Pause.*) Joseph.
> (*Shouting.*) Joseph!

> (*The* GOLEM, *sheepishly, like a
> child who knows he has done
> something wrong, slowly enters,
> head hanging.*)

I prayed to God for a miracle,
and my prayers were answered.
You've lived but a single day,
and look how quickly
the man in you has revealed himself.
Did I create you so you could be
like other men?
Answer me! Answer!

(*The* GOLEM *kneels before the* MAHARAL, *then lies prone at his feet.*)

Get up! I can see that you're sorry and asking my forgiveness! Of course I forgive you. Just don't do it again.

GOLEM. Then don't leave me!

MAHARAL. Stand up.

GOLEM. Let me lie here at your feet a little longer.

MAHARAL. Stand up!

GOLEM. One moment longer. I feel so good, so safe. (*Suddenly agitated and frightened. Standing. Gazing about.*)

MAHARAL. What's the matter? What do you see?

GOLEM. Next Passover!

MAHARAL. What about next Passover?

GOLEM. Blood and fire!
Mobs are coming
with torches, clubs, and knives.
Great flames blaze and leap,
and vicious dogs bark.
The sky lights up bright orange,
and on the earth,
blood flows everywhere.

MAHARAL. So next Passover they're coming to murder us again! But this time we have you to protect us! That is your destiny. That is your great mission. (*Pause.*) And now what do you see?

GOLEM. I no longer see blood and fire. I see nothing but darkness—darkness coming to the castle tower.

MAHARAL. You see the present. Go to the tower at once and stay there! When the priest comes to throw the homeless Jews out, frighten him off, but do not kill him. Now go!

> (*The* GOLEM *bounds out. The* MAHARAL *stands despondent.*)

> (*Fade-out.*)

Scene 5

That night. The castle tower in the Jewish quarter. Only the great room is visible. It is a shambles. It has doorways without doors, window frames without windows. The walls have cracks, missing chunks of plaster, sections covered with graffiti, and one section with a remnant of a mural. A lantern with a burning candle hangs from a hook on the wall. Cobwebs abound. YANKL is alone, sitting in a corner.

YANKL. (*Shivering.*) Where is everyone? (*Answering his own question.*) Still out begging. If I should die, who would care? (*Pause.*) How cold it is! If only I could get a bowl of hot soup. O God of Abraham, Isaac, and Jacob!

(*The GOLEM enters befuddled,
turning every which way.*)

(*Hearing the* GOLEM.)   Someone's come!
(*Seeing the* GOLEM.)   What are *you* doing
here?   This is a castle.   You belong in the
woodshed.   Where's your ax?   Why don't you
answer?   What do you want?   A place to sleep,
is that what you want?   That's why everyone
comes.

GOLEM.   Don't speak to me!

YANKL.   Woodcutter, are you a stranger to town?
Is this your first time in Prague?

GOLEM.   Don't speak to me!

(*The GOLEM wanders into the
hallway, out of sight. The* BLIND
MAN, *tapping and scanning with
an outstretched cane, and the*
REDHEAD *enter.*)

REDHEAD.   Do you understand what I've been
telling you?

BLIND MAN.   Everybody's been talking about it,
so it must be true.   They intend to throw us out
of here.   (*Alarmed.*)   Are we alone?

REDHEAD.   Yankl's over there, but I think he's
asleep.   Anyway, he's crazy.

BLIND MAN.   Isn't there someone else besides
him?

REDHEAD.   No.   He's the only one.

BLIND MAN. Are you sure? Look around—
carefully.

YANKL. In the hallway! Someone's there. A
stranger.

REDHEAD. A stranger? (*Peering through the
doorway and returning.*) It's the woodcutter!
The one—

BLIND MAN. —who grabbed Eva and kissed her?

REDHEAD. Yes.

BLIND MAN. What's he doing here? (*To the
REDHEAD.*) Maybe one of your customers?

YANKL. He came by himself. O God of Abraham,
Isaac, and Jacob!

REDHEAD. I hear he's a friend of the Maharal's.
Maybe the Maharal sent him here.

GOLEM. (*Appearing in the doorway.*) Who's
talking about me?

REDHEAD. No one. We only said—

GOLEM. I don't care what you said. Just don't
talk about me anymore! (*Returning to the
hallway.*)

YANKL. O God of Abraham, Isaac, and Jacob!

(*The* BLONDE *enters.*)

BLONDE. (*To the* REDHEAD.) Hi, Rosie. (*To
ALL.*) Hi, everyone.

ALL. Hi, Blondie.

REDHEAD. Blondie, we have a guest here.

BLONDE. Guest? What guest?

REDHEAD. The woodcutter from the shul
courtyard.

BLONDE. Really? All Prague is talking about him.

REDHEAD. (*Pointing.*) He's sitting over there in the dark.

BLONDE. What's he doing there?

REDHEAD. I think he's hiding. The Maharal sent him here.

BLONDE. What's his name?

REDHEAD. Joseph. And he's enormous! Just your type!

BLONDE. I have no type—and no family either. When I was little, the priest gave me the choice he gave every orphaned Jewish girl—to convert and be fed by the church—and (*Slowly, ironically.*) be cared for by him—or to live as a Jew as best I could. He gave you the same choice, so you should know better than to make fun of me.

REDHEAD. I wasn't making fun of you. Just joking.

(*The* GOLEM *strides in.*)

GOLEM. Who called me?

REDHEAD. I just mentioned your name. I didn't *call* you.

GOLEM. Don't say my name again! I've already told you once. (*Returning to the hallway.*)

REDHEAD. Is there a law that says you can't say a man's name?

YANKL. Every good-for-nothing ends up here. O God of Abraham, Isaac, and Jacob!

REDHEAD. Blondie, you didn't see the priest on your way here?

BLONDE. No. Why?

REDHEAD. They want to drive us out.

BLONDE. From ruins? They throw people from their homes, but who's ever heard of throwing people from ruins?

REDHEAD. (*Ironically.*) We are the envy of Prague because we live in a castle.

BLIND MAN. What if they come and ask for everything we own?

REDHEAD. Well, we open our sacks and pour out all the silver coins, and then we gaze about this magnificent room and say, "Take everything! It's yours!"

BLIND MAN. There is a God in heaven, Jews!

YANKL. Of course there's a God in heaven,
and he looks after the Jews
and all who suffer.
He looks after the beggars and the poor,
the sick, the deaf, the blind,
and he looks after the whores
and the homeless,
and the persecuted, the oppressed,
the anxious and distressed,
the lame, the insane, those in pain,
and all who sorrow
with no hope of tomorrow.

ALL. There is a God in heaven,
and he looks after us all.

YANKL. Elijah didn't come today.
And neither did the Messiah.

Maybe they'll come tomorrow
or the next day.

BLIND MAN. It's not too late. They might still
come today.

YANKL. O God of Abraham, Isaac, and Jacob!
I've been lying here all day.
The one I always call upon
is not the one who came.
But the one I did not call upon
is the one who came.

BLIND MAN. What's he saying? I don't
understand a word of it.

YANKL. I'll explain it to you: I call upon the
Messiah all the time, but he never comes. I
didn't call upon that giant in the hall, but he
came.

ALL. There is a God in heaven, and he looks after
us all.

(*The* GOLEM *appears in the
doorway.* YANKL *walks up to him
and bursts out laughing.*)

BLONDE. What are you laughing at, you crazy
fool?

YANKL. (*To the* GOLEM.) Do you know them?
Are they friends of yours?
Do you know what they do?
No, I don't think you do.
Well, listen to me:
I am in charge here.
Beat them up!

Trample them!
They are homeless.
They are good-for-nothings!
They are the scum of the earth!
But you! You're a somebody!
You are a woodcutter,
and you have an ax.
Take care of them!

GOLEM. I obey only the Maharal.

> (*The* GOLEM *disappears into the
> hallway.* YANKL *sits on the floor,
> holds his head in his hands, and
> begins to twitch.*)

REDHEAD. (*Looking at* YANKL.) Nuttier
   than a fruitcake!
BLONDE. All you have to do is get him started!
YANKL. (*Suddenly standing, then prancing.*)
   Just remember this and never forget it!
   I am master here!
   The broken windows are all mine.
   The doorways without doors are all mine.
   And no one gains admittance
   unless I say so! (*Pause.*)
   And when my guests come,
   Elijah the Prophet, in his chariot of fire,
   bringing his friend the Messiah,
   you will all have to go. (*Pause.*)
   Should I put on my party clothes?
   Should I sweep the floor, wash the dishes,
   polish the silver?

Take from their places all the treasure—
the candlesticks, china, crystal—
and spread on the table
a cloth of purest white? (*Pause.*)
The guest of honor
is bringing the wine. (*Pause.*)
Have I forgotten something?
Is this a catered affair?
Where are the servants and attendants
standing ready in their finest array
at all the doors?
Where are the musicians and dancers?
(*Shouting.*) Servants, do you hear?
Get ready for the party.

> (*The two* WANDERERS *enter, one
> old, the other young. They wear
> robes and carry staffs—the very
> picture of prophets as imagined
> from the Hebrew Scriptures.*)

But look who's coming!
None other than my honored guests from afar!
Surely you know who they are!
WANDERERS. (*Together.*) Good evening, Jews.
ALL. Good evening, strangers.
OLD WANDERER. Jews, can we spend the night?
REDHEAD. Of course, Your Grace!
OLD WANDERER. We'll only spend one night!
REDHEAD. (*Seductively.*) My Lord, you can stay
as long as you like. These ruins can
accommodate us all.

OLD WANDERER. Thank you,
   but one night will do.
   My friend is tired,
   and his feet hurt, too.
   We've been hurrying.
YANKL. He's tired and his feet hurt!
   (*Aside.*) What kind of messiah is this?
   (*Sitting, dejected, twitching.*)
REDHEAD. You've come to Prague for a reason?
   You need something here?
OLD WANDERER. Yes, we've come for a reason.
   And we need one night's sleep. (*Pause.*)
   What's new in Prague?
REDHEAD. The news is not good, sweetheart.
OLD WANDERER. Not good?
BLONDE. No, not good for the Jews. But your
   friend, the young one—he doesn't look like
   any beggar I've ever seen. His features are so
   fine. To tell the truth, he's cute.
REDHEAD. (*To the* OLD WANDERER.) Tell
   me, darling, have you come from far away?
OLD WANDERER. From very far away.
   From the desert of *EH-retz YISS-rah-ale,*
   the Land of Israel.
   Today we arrived at the border of this town
   just as the sun went down.
   We saw in the distance this old castle,
   and we came here and looked—
   broken windows, no doors.
   It was our kind of place,
   so we entered.

(*Pointing to* YANKL, *who is still sitting and twitching.*)

That one over there, what's the matter with him?

REDHEAD. He's crazy.

YOUNG WANDERER. I'm so tired.

> (YOUNG WANDERER *lies on the floor.* OLD WANDERER *places some rags under* YOUNG WANDERER *'s head.*)

OLD WANDERER. Sleep well, my friend, sleep well.

YANKL. (*Suddenly standing.*)
  What's the meaning of this!
  Strangers come to spend the night.
  You treat them like guests.
  And no one asks my permission!
  I'm still boss here!

REDHEAD. Shut up! Can't you see the young man is trying to sleep!

YANKL. Wake him up! No one sleeps here! This is a place for vigil and trembling, a place to wait for the Messiah. When he comes, the dead will awake, rise, and sing.

REDHEAD. You're a madman! Shut up!

(*The* MAHARAL *enters hurriedly.*)

ALL. (*In surprise.*) The Maharal!

BLIND MAN. Maharal, we have visitors! Yankl
    says they're Elijah and the Messiah.
YANKL. Maharal, can the Messiah be tired?
    Can the Messiah have sore feet?
MAHARAL. (*Scrutinizing the* WANDERERS.
    Dubious about their identity. To the OLD
    WANDERER.)
    Is it *you,* Elijah?
    It can't be you.
    Can it be *you*?
    I don't believe it!
    If it is you, why are you here?
    Why have you come?
    Why did you bring *him*?
    Who sent for you?
    This isn't your moment!
    We don't need you now!
    We have a golem to protect us.
    I couldn't wait for you any longer!
    Go!
OLD WANDERER. We've come only for the
    night. Tomorrow we'll be on our way.
MAHARAL. What are you talking about! Get him
    up at once! Wake him up and go! You must
    not tarry!
OLD WANDERER. But we are exhausted from
    hurrying so! Only one night, please, I beg of
    you!
MAHARAL. You hurried here? Well, hurry away!
OLD WANDERER. (*Pointing to the* YOUNG
    WANDERER *sound asleep, breathing deeply*.)
    He sleeps so soundly. Don't wake him.

MAHARAL. Are there no ruins elsewhere in the world? You have to sleep here? Only here? Wake him up! You come unbidden! I forbid it! Joseph!

> (*The* GOLEM *enters. The* OLD WANDERER *is frightened and prods the sleeping* YOUNG WANDERER *with his staff.*)

OLD WANDERER. Wake up! Wake up! We have to go! (*Scrutinizing the* GOLEM.) We've got to go!

YOUNG WANDERER. A little longer! Just let me sleep a little longer! Yankl says I'm the Messiah. Don't you care about the Messiah? (*Falling back asleep.*)

YANKL. (*To the* OLD WANDERER.) Are you from Gilead?

OLD WANDERER. Yes! How did you know?

YANKL. What about him? Is he from Bethlehem?

OLD WANDERER. Yes. He's spent most of his life there.

YANKL. So he's not from Nazareth?

OLD WANDERER. No, he's never been there.

YANKL. (*Pointing to the* YOUNG WANDERER.)
You, young wanderer,
whom I want to believe in so much!
(*Then looking around the room for someone else.*) And you, too,
Jesus of Nazareth,
the Jew who is worshipped by the Gentiles,

(*Still searching the room.*)
wherever, whatever, whoever you are!
Two messiahs are better than one.
I'd gladly believe in you both!
And if a third messiah should come along,
I'd believe in him, too! (*Pause.*)
Only tell me, tell me true,
when is there going to be
peace on earth, goodwill to men? (*Pause.*)
For us, there's only sorrow,
no end of pain.
Perhaps all that will change tomorrow
after tonight's rain.

     (*The* GOLEM *walks up close to the*
     WANDERERS.)

OLD WANDERER. (*Terrified. Prodding harder.*)
    Get up! Get up! We have to go!
    We're not wanted here!
MAHARAL. Go! Go now! If you wait a moment
    longer, it may be too late.
OLD WANDERER. But the road is so dark.
MAHARAL. Yes, of course. It's nighttime.
    Why did you bring him here?
    What can he do for us
    except make promises he cannot fulfill—
    just like all the others? (*Pause.*)
    The world is still cruel and full of pain,
    so take him and go away!
    Escape while you can!
    Soon there will be bloodshed.

There's only one who can help us now.
(*Pointing to the* GOLEM.) Him!

YOUNG WANDERER. (*Standing.*) I want
to stop all murder,
to bring an end to hate and suffering,
and forever abolish war.
That's what a messiah is for.
Instead, I'm told
by every Christian and Jew—
and everyone else, too—
that I'm not wanted, to leave,
to get out of town as quickly as I can.
And so I hurry and scurry
from place to place
and never get to tarry.

OLD WANDERER. It seems we always come
before our time.
Let's go back to the desert
and wait for the call to come.

YOUNG WANDERER. But we've been waiting
almost forever.

OLD WANDERER. My friend, that's not long.

MAHARAL. Yes, return to the desert. If you
stay, you'll soon hear the sound of marching
feet, the tramping of boots.

OLD WANDERER. What feet, what boots?

MAHARAL. The enemy's!
Right before Easter,
they'll come again to destroy us,
saying we've killed one of their children
to get blood for our Passover celebration.
You must escape while there's still time.

YOUNG WANDERER. But Passover's not until
    spring.
MAHARAL. Blood knows no season! Now go!
YANKL. (*Imperiously.*) Wait a moment!
    Tell me, Wise Men, before you go,
    what comes after the grave?
    Surely you know.
    Resurrection for our bodies?
    Or heaven for our souls?
    Which is it? Or is it both?
    (*Laughing.*) What's the difference?
    Just a pretext, just a hoax
    for all the fools who like their jokes!
    (*Suddenly dancing and singing.*)
    So sing a song of nonsense.
    Sing a song of madness.
    Sing a song of nothing. (*Stopping abruptly.
    Turning to the* WANDERERS.)
    Now you may go.

        (*The* WANDERERS *leave.*)

    So off they go, never daring to tarry.
    Not with honor do we greet our guests,
    not with joy, not with a blessing.
    We did not offer them a roof for their head,
    nor a glass of water, nor a morsel of bread.
    Why, we didn't even say good-bye.
    They're gone, gone, gone.
    And they may never come this way again.
    (*Laughing.*)

(*The* GOLEM *starts to exit in the direction of the* WANDERERS, *but the* MAHARAL *blocks him.*)

MAHARAL. (*To the* GOLEM.)   Where do you
   think you're going?
GOLEM.   With them!   I want to go with them,
   with Elijah and the Messiah!   Let me go!
MAHARAL.   No!   You cannot go with them.
   You must stay.
   Their moment has not yet come!
   This is *your* moment!
   The priest will be here soon.

(ALL *become agitated.*)

BLIND MAN.   What does he want with us?
MAHARAL.   He wants to drive you out.   This old
   castle doesn't belong to you.
YANKL.   Soon they will be gone.
   Gone, gone, gone.
MAHARAL.   (*To the* GOLEM.)   You know what
   you have to do?
GOLEM.   I know, Maharal.
MAHARAL.   Frighten them,
   but do not kill them.
   "Thou shalt not murder."
   That is the commandment.
   Do you understand?
GOLEM.   I understand, Maharal.
MAHARAL.   Well, then, go back to your place in
   the hall and wait.   I'm going to run and catch

up with the strangers and escort them safely
out of town. It's so dark outside. I don't want
them wandering back here by mistake.

(*The* GOLEM *returns to the hallway
as the* MAHARAL *exits*.)

YANKL. Gone, gone, gone.

(*The* OLD PRIEST *enters with the*
YOUNG PRIEST.)

OLD PRIEST. (*Scrutinizing all. Then, to the*
YOUNG PRIEST.)
Do you see these homeless Jews?
They're pretenders, every one! Charlatans!
Believe me, any one of them
is wealthier than both of us together!
Did you ever hear of a poor Jew? (*Pause*.)
On our way here, did you see the one
with the hump on his back?
The hump is false.
There are no Jews with humps.
That's where he stores his treasure,
wrapped in rags.
YOUNG PRIEST. If that is so, he's an artist.
OLD PRIEST. (*Pointing to the* BLIND MAN.)
And you see the one with the stick,
the blind one, over there?
He isn't blind at all!
Those eyes see very well.
You've never seen a blind Jew—

except in matters of religion!
Why, the Jews have eyes
in the back of their heads!
Their vision is so acute
they can see through walls
and right through people.

YOUNG PRIEST. Well, Father, in the city,
I saw a sincere Jew. He had only one arm.
You can't fake that.

OLD PRIEST. Don't you believe it!
They can fake anything!
His kind can amputate an arm
and keep it hidden in a sack,
and when he needs it,
take it out and use it,
good as new.

YOUNG PRIEST. Well, Father,
what about the whores? Are they fake, too?

OLD PRIEST. No. They're real enough.
(*Pause*.) Look at these people!
They hang around like lords,
as if they owned the place!
To think faithful noblemen and ladies
once lived here in splendor and glory!
And now all has gone to rack and ruin,
filled with mice and rats and Jews.

(*To* ALL.) Why do you stand
and gape at us in silence?
Haven't we tortured you enough?
Oppressed you enough?
Burnt you alive at the stake?

Led you out to slaughter?
We never grow weary
of our hatred and fury.
Yet you flaunt your religion before us
so flagrantly, so tenaciously,
constantly thwarting our efforts
to show you the way.
We hound you incessantly,
but you never seem to understand
that all we want for you (*Pause.*)
is *love*.

You say we accuse you falsely.
If you are innocent, as you claim,
why don't you attack us?
That's what we would do!
But not you, you cowards!
Even now as I speak,
not one of you has had the courage
to answer me.
Not one seizes me by the neck
or grabs a staff and bashes in my skull.
You just stand there, saying nothing,
doing nothing.
That's how you people behave!
No wonder we have contempt for you!
(*Spitting.*)
And you always wait
for me to shout, "Get out!"
And you're always ready to leave.
Well, then, (*Clapping his hands,
then shouting.*) go!

(ALL *stumble over one another as
they rush out*.)

(*Chuckling*.) Dogs!
Give the command,
and they obey! (*Reflecting*.)
But this is child's play.
Our work with these people
(*Menacingly, slowly*.) isn't over yet.
It won't be over
until we get rid of them all—
one way or another.

(*Soft footsteps*.)

Do you hear that? Footsteps.
Is one of them still here?
YOUNG PRIEST. No, they're all gone.
No one's here, Father.
OLD PRIEST. (*Momentarily dashing about and
searching*.) No one? But don't you hear
footsteps?
YOUNG PRIEST. It's your imagination, Father.
OLD PRIEST. But I *do* hear footsteps.
Surely you must, too!

(*By now the footsteps have grown
loud*.)

YOUNG PRIEST. *Now* I do! This place is
haunted! Evil spirits!

(*The* GOLEM *enters menacingly. Lightning flashes, lighting up the room. The* PRIESTS *see him.*)

Let's run, Father!

(*The* PRIESTS *run out. The* GOLEM *stands fierce and motionless. Lightning flashes again, followed by a clap of thunder, then a sudden downpour.*)

GOLEM. I came here to have a place to sleep with lots of company. (*Pause.*)
But I'm all alone. (*Slowly lying down and falling asleep. The downpour is torrential.*)

(*Fade-out.*)

INTERMISSION

ACT II

Scene 1

That night, a couple of hours later. The castle tower. The GOLEM *is sleeping.* YANKL, *drenched by the rain, enters and shakes off the rain, not noticing the* GOLEM.

YANKL. (*To himself.*) Such a downpour! I was driven out of here before the storm. I wandered down many streets and alleys, but no one anywhere let me in. So I came back here, where the doors are always open.
(*Looking about.*) But there's no one here! Gone, gone, gone.
(*Suddenly laughing, then clamping his hands over his mouth to stifle the laughter.*)

59

Maybe everyone's dead.
Maybe that's why
they didn't open a single door.
If all are dead, there are no more.
Why didn't I think of that before?

(*Lightning lights up the room and
the sleeping* GOLEM. *A clap of
thunder wakes him. He rubs his
eyes and sits.*)

A survivor! The only one! Who are you?

GOLEM. You know!

YANKL. No, I don't. If everyone is dead, you
must be dead, too!

GOLEM. I'm alive. I'm the one assigned to guard
this place and protect the people.

YANKL. Some protector! You let the priests
drive us out. And now everyone's dead.
Gone, gone, gone.

GOLEM. I didn't know they were going to drive
you out until after they did it.

YANKL. Yes, you're right. That's the paradox of
protection. You have to wait for the enemy to
strike before you can defend yourself.

GOLEM. Well, I frightened them off. And if
anyone needs help, I'll give it.

(EVA*'s voice is heard shouting
"Help!"*)

YANKL. You didn't have to wait long!
There's lots going on today.

First, Elijah comes, bringing the Messiah!
Then the homeless are thrown out of here!
Then everyone's dead!
And now someone's crying for help!
That's too much excitement
for Yankl in a single day.
I'm going to have to find another place
to rest my head.

> (YANKL *runs out.* EVA*'s voice
> again shouts "Help!" The* GOLEM
> *goes to his hiding place in the
> hallway. After a moment,* PEARL
> *and* EVA *enter, frightened and
> clinging to each other.*)

EVA. (*Shouting.*) Grampa!
PEARL. We're out of our minds
to come out in weather like this!
Now we're hopelessly lost
in this maze of an old castle
looking for your grandfather,
and nothing will come
from shouting "Help!"
EVA. But we must find him.
It's not like him to be away so long.
Grampa! Grampa!
PEARL. Maharal! Maharal!
There must be a doorway somewhere
that leads to the outside.

> (*The* GOLEM *steps into the room.
> Lightning flashes. The* WOMEN

*see him and cry out in terror. A
clap of thunder.*)

GOLEM. You cried for help. You're lost.
    So why do you scream
    when I intend to help you
    and show you the way out?
PEARL. Leave us alone!
GOLEM. Who else do you think will come?
    I'm the only one
    who can help you,
    and you send me away.
PEARL. Have you seen the Maharal?
    He said he was coming here,
    but that was several hours ago.
GOLEM. The Maharal was here,
    but he's not here now.
PEARL. Where did he go? He didn't come home.
GOLEM. He went to escort
    Elijah the Prophet
    and the Messiah out of town.
    Their moment has not yet come.
    (*Proudly.*) This is my moment.
EVA. (*To* PEARL.) What's he talking about?
PEARL. I don't have the faintest idea. He's as
    crazy as Yankl.

    (*Flash of lightning, clap of
    thunder.*)

EVA. (*Gazing into the* GOLEM*'s eyes. Aside.*)
    He's such a big man! (*To* PEARL.) Gramma,
    we've got to go back home!

GOLEM. (*To* EVA.)
    Eva, when you look into my eyes,
    I remember that moment
    when I embraced you,
    pressed you close to me,
    felt the warmth of your body next to mine,
    the thrill of your cheek against mine,
    your breast trembling against me.
    But then I could not speak,
    could not even catch my breath. (*Pause.*)
    It's different now.
    It's enough for me to gaze
    on your beautiful face.
    And yet, if I wished,
    I could take you in my arms
    and press my yearning lips against yours.

        (PEARL *and* EVA *look on in
        horror and astonishment.*)

I'm dazzled by my own words
that dance so nimbly off my tongue.
There is more that I could say:
I could toss you over my shoulder
and through the storm's flashing
carry you to another part of the castle.

        (*Crash of lightning, clap of
        thunder.*)

And I would see the wind waft your clothing
and the lightning reveal your body,
and feel the empty room overflow

with your warmth,
our skins against each other
evoking more excitement
than the flashing lightning in the skies.
I would kiss your limbs,
and we would entwine together as one.
And afterwards
we would huddle in the stillness. (*Pause.*)

I am ashamed by all the things I said.
I revealed to you the secrets of my heart.
When I heard you calling in the ruins,
it was the most happy sound I'd ever heard.
Now all has grown quiet. (*Pause.*)
But, see how you are trembling!
We should lie down somewhere
but dare not. (*Pause.*)
One day soon, houses will be burning
and falling in the fires,
and people dying—
to the music of church bells joyously ringing.
But I see you somewhere safe,
slumbering in peace,
a peace that I have created.

(*Walking about happily, almost dancing.*)
See how far and wide my arms can spread.
Even my strides take wing!
Every gesture brings me joy.
Come, frightened and bewildered women,
let us go. I'll lead the way.
Come! Follow me!

(PEARL *and* EVA *are in a trance. The* GOLEM *extends his hand.* PEARL *takes it, and he slowly leads them out.*)

(*Fade-out.*)

Scene 2

That night, a little later. The castle tower. The GOLEM *returns alone, sits down, and proceeds to rock, his hands crossed over his chest.*

GOLEM. When they cried for help,
    didn't I respond?
    Weren't they hoping
    someone would come?
    Weren't they counting on me,
    or did they expect another?
    O walls of my castle tower,
    why are you so silent?

    (YANKL *enters.*)

YANKL. Who is our savior? Our protector?
    Who?
GOLEM. I am!
YANKL. *You*? (*Laughing out loud.*)
    Ha! Ha! Ha!
GOLEM. Don't laugh! Don't talk!

YANKL. So look who's telling Yankl not to talk!

(*The* GOLEM *frowns threateningly.*)

All right! I'll be quiet.

(*The* GOLEM *sits. After a moment*
YANKL *sits a few feet away from*
him.)

GOLEM. Move closer!

(YANKL *slides closer.*)

Closer!

(YANKL *slides next to the*
GOLEM, *and the* GOLEM *puts an*
arm around YANKL*'s shoulder.*)

That's good.
That's the way friends sit,
I've noticed.
YANKL. Yes.
GOLEM. I feel happy here. You, too?
YANKL. Yes.
GOLEM. I love these walls—walls I can call my
own. Do you feel that way, too?
YANKL. Yes. The walls you speak of are called
"home."
GOLEM. Home. Everyone needs to have one. I
bet it's nice when there's someone who waits
there for you and greets you.

YANKL. Yes.
GOLEM. I miss the others. Do you?
YANKL. Yes.
GOLEM. The Maharal is on his way here.
   I wonder whether he feels that way, too.
YANKL. No. This isn't the Maharal's home.
GOLEM. (*Angrily pushing* YANKL *away.*)
   Move away! And stay away!

> (*The* GOLEM *lies down on the floor
> and falls asleep, breathing deeply.
> YANKL stands and tiptoes out.
> After a moment, the* MAHARAL
> *enters. He sees the* GOLEM.)

MAHARAL. Wake up! Get up! It's time!
GOLEM. (*Waking.*) Maharal!
   You're drenched. And I'm cold and wet.
MAHARAL. It's been raining.
   It's been raining in on you.
GOLEM. Where am I, Maharal?
MAHARAL. You don't know?
   In the castle tower.
GOLEM. I must have fallen asleep,
   and when you came in,
   I must have been dreaming.
MAHARAL. What were you dreaming?
GOLEM. I dreamt a stillness
   and darkness
   came over me.
   Then you dragged me by my legs
   to a pit.
   You threw me in

and began to shovel earth over me.
You were burying me.
Suddenly a woman began to weep—
Eva!—
yes, I'm sure it was Eva.
MAHARAL. Who?
GOLEM. She was seized with sobbing.
And she fell on me and embraced me,
both her hands pressing against my breast,
and she wept and would not stop weeping.
And through her sobs, she kissed me
and cried over and over again,
"I love you"
until you told her to climb out,
and she did.
She stood by your side
and continued to weep,
and you were weeping, too.
Then you said, "How foolish we are
to mourn a golem,
to mourn a lump of clay."
MAHARAL. Darkness and wild terror
have possessed you.
Come. I need you.
GOLEM. (*Standing.*) Here I am, Maharal.
I'm ready.
Tell me what I must do.
MAHARAL. You must leave this place and return
to the courtyard. You need to chop wood.
GOLEM. Don't ask me to do that. I want to stay
here forever.
MAHARAL. That's impossible.
Your whole purpose

is to wait for the moments
when I need you.
That is your destiny.
Soon you will have another mission.
So you must come with me.
Come!

(*They slowly exit. After a moment,*
YANKL enters.)

YANKL. (*Forlorn.*) Save us! Save us!
Who is going to save us?
Who is going to protect us? (*Long pause.*)
Who?

(*He starts to exit, and the lights*
begin to fade. Then he stops and
turns to the audience.)

Who?

(*Fade-out.*)

Scene 3

A few days later. It is Friday afternoon, shortly
before sunset and the onset of the Sabbath. The
courtyard of the shul. The action begins in the
woodshed in the courtyard. The woodshed has
imaginary walls and an imaginary door. In the
woodshed, on one side, are a mat—the burlap

blanket of Act I, scene 2, which is now the
GOLEM's bed—and a bench; at the end of the
bench are a pitcher of water and a cup. On the
other side of the woodshed are stacked wood and
the same ax that appeared in Act I, scene 4.

The space outside the woodshed is the
courtyard, which fills the remainder of the stage.

The main doorway to the shul is imagined to
be located in the center aisle, just in front of the
stage. The side doorway is upstage. The shul itself
is not seen at all. Most of the congregation (the
audience) has already gathered in the shul for
"Welcoming the Sabbath," which precedes the
Sabbath service and the Sabbath itself. Two
stragglers, BASHEVI and YANKL, have yet to
appear.

When the lights come up, the GOLEM,
shabby, unkempt, and wearing one shoe, is lying
on the mat. His other shoe lies close to the bench.
After a moment, BASHEVI enters the courtyard on
his way to shul. On seeing the GOLEM through the
open door of the woodshed, he enters the
woodshed.

BASHEVI. (*Annoyed.*) Hey, woodcutter! What
     are you doing lying on your bed? Why aren't
     you ready to go to shul to greet the Sabbath?
     (*Pause.*) Tell me, are you a Jew?
GOLEM. No.
BASHEVI. Are you a Gentile?
GOLEM. No.
BASHEVI. Not a Jew, not a Gentile. But you have
     to be one or the other! So what are you?

GOLEM. I don't know.

BASHEVI. You don't know! (*Puzzled.*) Is there a prayer for someone who doesn't know? (*Noticing that the* GOLEM *has only one shoe on.*) Where's your other shoe? You need to wear two shoes to greet the Sabbath.

GOLEM. Shoe? What shoe?

BASHEVI. What do you mean, "What shoe?" *Your* shoe, not *mine*! You must wear shoes on the Sabbath!

GOLEM. But I am wearing a shoe, can't you see?

BASHEVI. What's the use of talking to you!

GOLEM. Well, find my other shoe and give it to me, and I'll put it on.

BASHEVI. *Find* your shoe? *Give* it to you? What am I, your servant?

GOLEM. Well, if you don't want to, don't!

BASHEVI. You can't go to shul and pray without two shoes on. (*Pause.*) Are you deaf?

GOLEM. I don't know how to pray.

BASHEVI. You are a savage! You should be sent away! Why don't you wash yourself?

GOLEM. Go away and leave me alone! Send the Maharal here! I want the Maharal!

BASHEVI. Get up and come to shul! Wash your face!

GOLEM. It's been several days since the Maharal came to see me.

BASHEVI. Why should the Maharal come to see you? Who are *you*?

GOLEM. He has cast me completely aside.

BASHEVI. I don't know what you're talking about. Last night you kept me awake. You

bellowed and cried, you sobbed and wept all
through the night. No one could sleep.

GOLEM. (*Sitting up.*) Tonight I will not cry.
Tonight I will be quiet.

BASHEVI. That's what you said yesterday.

GOLEM. Tonight I will be quiet. Now I must get
dressed. My shoe. Where is my shoe?
(*Searching for his shoe, he finds it and tries to
put it on without success. Angrily he hurls it
across the room.*) Send the Maharal here! Tell
him I need him to put on my shoe!

BASHEVI. You need the Maharal to put on your
shoe?

GOLEM. Why do you repeat what I say? Can't
you hear? *Are you deaf?* (*Jumping up.*) Go
and tell him that I want him! Tell the Maharal
that Joseph wants him!

BASHEVI. Such impudence! I've never heard the
likes of it. You are a madman!

GOLEM. (*Springing at* BASHEVI.) I told you to
go! (*Menacingly.*) Go!

> (BASHEVI, *terrified, runs out,
> crosses the courtyard, and enters
> the shul. The* GOLEM *sits on his
> bench.* YANKL *crosses the
> courtyard. On seeing the* GOLEM
> *through the open doorway, he
> enters the woodshed.*)

YANKL. (*To the* GOLEM, *cheerfully.*) Get ready
for shul.

GOLEM. The Maharal told me to wait here. He cooped me up here. And he doesn't come to see me.

YANKL. Perhaps you said something wrong to him, something that made him angry?

> (*At this suggestion the* GOLEM *bellows.* YANKL *turns to the audience.*)

Suffering, even of the innocent,
is the inescapable lot of man.
To endure suffering is to be a hero.
To have compassion for the suffering
is to be like God.

> (*Kneeling and lifting the* GOLEM*'s shoe and offering it to him.*)

Here, my friend, is your shoe.

GOLEM. Get out of here!

YANKL. (*Carefully setting down the shoe, then standing.*) Did you hear that the castle tower is vacant? No one's there. All the doors are boarded up, and the windows, too.

GOLEM. Then I'll go there at once and rip the boards off!

YANKL. Someone will only board them up again. Besides, no one sleeps there anymore.

GOLEM. I'm going there anyway.
I won't stay here.
The castle tower is empty? No.
Someone sits there and waits for me.

YANKL. Who is waiting for you?

GOLEM. I thought I heard him calling. (*Pause.*)
No, you're here, so you can't be there.
You're right. There's no one there.
Get away from me! Get out of here!

> (*He rushes at* YANKL *with raised fists. Just then the* MAHARAL *enters the woodshed.*)

MAHARAL. Do not raise your hand!
Do not make a fist!

GOLEM. (*Hanging his head in shame as he lowers his arms and unclenches his fists. Then lifting his head and exclaiming joyously.*)
Oh, Maharal, I'm so happy to see you!

MAHARAL. Against whom did you
raise your hand?

GOLEM. (*Stammering.*) Against Yankl.
(*Turning to* YANKL.) Yankl, I'm sorry.

YANKL. It's all right.
You didn't mean it.

MAHARAL. Yankl, go to the shul.

> (YANKL *leaves the woodshed and enters the shul.*)

I understand you want to see me.

> (*The* GOLEM *does not reply.*)

What do you want? (*Pause.*)
Why don't you answer?

You told everyone you wanted to see me.
(*Pause.*) You are practically barefoot.

GOLEM. Day and night I wait for you to come.
I think every sound is a sign of your coming.
And then, no sooner do you appear
than you go.
You look at me, then you turn
and leave me alone as before.
Stay with me. I want your nearness,
just your nearness, nothing more.

MAHARAL. You must get used to being alone.
You ought to be waiting expectantly
for those moments when I need you
rather than yearning for me and needing me.

GOLEM. You have abandoned me.

MAHARAL. No, I have not! (*Pause.*)
Unwashed, unkempt!
And I hear that you lie awake all night and cry.

GOLEM. I can't sleep. I'm afraid.

MAHARAL. What are you afraid of?

GOLEM. Of my right arm.

MAHARAL. (*Puzzled.*) Of your right arm?

GOLEM. Of what it might do.
It's very large and very strong. (*Pause.*)
I've come to understand everything,
and I can see that you don't need me.

MAHARAL. Of course, I need you.
What do you mean?

GOLEM. You never come to see me anymore.
Why do you torture me so?

MAHARAL. You don't seem to understand that I
gave you freedom, except for the moments
when I need you.

GOLEM. No, you didn't! You cooped me up here.

MAHARAL. I permitted you to come and go. You chose to stay. You have forgotten.

GOLEM. Where can I go, when you hold me fast within your grasp, but you're not with me?

MAHARAL. I'm with you now.

GOLEM. Stay with me forever. I'll give you my bed. (*Pointing to his mat.*) You can sleep on it, and I'll sleep on the floor at your feet.

MAHARAL. You are so restless—and so helpless. But who can blame you? You had no childhood. I was certain that you would find yourself, find peace, and start to live as all Jews live, as all people live.

GOLEM. But you never taught me.

MAHARAL. I see that you can't get rid of your helplessness. And so you want me to give up the world, to leave it and remain here with you. And if I do that, what then?

GOLEM. My restlessness would leave me.

MAHARAL. Unrest is your fate.
    It is man's fate. (*Pause.*)
    I must go now. (*The* MAHARAL *takes a few steps toward the courtyard.*)

GOLEM. (*Standing.*) Do not forsake me.

MAHARAL. The congregation is waiting for me to lead them in prayer.

GOLEM. Don't go to them.
    If you don't want to stay with me,
    then let me return to the castle tower.

MAHARAL. The tower is closed. Forever.

GOLEM. Forever?

MAHARAL. Forever. (*Again starting to go.*)

GOLEM. Don't go!

> (*He grabs the* MAHARAL *by the arm.*)

MAHARAL. Let go! I must go! They're waiting for me!

GOLEM. Stay! I say stay!

MAHARAL. And so you give me orders now? You command me?

GOLEM. Yes. I command you to stay.

MAHARAL. Is it your lips that speak these words?

GOLEM. Yes, *my* lips. And (*Holding up his right hand.*) do you see this hand? (*Making a fist threateningly.*) It's *mine*, too.

MAHARAL. (*Without flinching.*) Lower your arm, relax your fist, and let go of me.

> (*The* GOLEM *slowly lets go. When released, the* MAHARAL *turns his back on the* GOLEM, *leaves the woodshed, walks across the courtyard, and enters the shul. The service of "Welcoming the Sabbath" can be heard, with the congregation joyfully singing* "L'CHKAH doe-DEE."
>
> *As the singing continues, the* GOLEM *sits on his bench, holds his head in his hands, and then lets out a prolonged and sorrowful bellow followed by sobbing.*

He stops sobbing and lifts his head. After a moment, he spots his shoe, picks it up, puts it on, and laces it up competently and resolutely. He pours some water from the pitcher into the cup, takes a gulp, and splashes the rest across his face. He walks to the corner of the woodshed where the ax stands, picks it up, then goes back to the bench and sits down, examining and fondling the ax.)

GOLEM. (*Muttering angrily, barely audible at first, then increasing to a frenzy of rage.*)
I'm a stranger and a guest . . .
I'm welcome but shouldn't speak . . .
I can't look at her, can't talk to her,
can't touch her . . . I hate them!
And him most of all! . . . I'm his slave
and his prisoner, but he says I'm free . . .
(*Mockingly.*) No, Joseph! No, Joseph! . . .
Woodcutter! Protector! Savior! . . .
Golem! Golem! . . . Here I am!
Here I am!
(*Lifting the ax, standing,
shouting like a battle cry.*)

Hee-NAY-nee!

(*Charging toward the shul with continued cries.*)

(*"L'CHKAH doe-DEE" is still being sung, louder and more joyously than before. After a moment, the singing is interrupted by the sounds of people screaming, followed by crashing glass and the smashing of walls, then people groaning, moaning, and wailing. BASHEVI and YANKL come rushing from the side doorway of the shul into the courtyard.*)

YANKL. What happened?

BASHEVI. Couldn't you see from where you were sitting? The woodcutter with his ax went berserk. At least one is dead, and many are wounded.

YANKL. (*Weeping.*) Who will save us?

Who will protect us? (*Gazing heavenward.*)

(YANKL *continues to weep and sob, while* BASHEVI *has a blank stare. After a moment, the* MAHARAL *comes out of the side doorway of the shul, leading the* GOLEM *by his left hand, the* GOLEM *holding the bloody ax in his right. The* MAHARAL *takes the ax from the* GOLEM *and turns to* BASHEVI *and* YANKL.)

MAHARAL. Everything's all right now.
    Everything's under control.
    The wounded are being cared for.
    Go back to the shul
    and tell the congregation
    that everything's all right
    and to resume the service.

> (*The* MAHARAL *leads the* GOLEM
> *toward the woodshed.* YANKL *is*
> *weeping, and* BASHEVI *is without*
> *emotion as they go to the main*
> *doorway of the shul.*)

BASHEVI. (*Shouting into the shul.*)
    The Maharal says everything's all right now!
    Resume the service.

> (BASHEVI *and* YANKL *enter the*
> *shul. The service resumes with a*
> *markedly subdued singing of*
> "L'CHKAH   doe-DEE." *The*
> MAHARAL *and the* GOLEM *enter*
> *the woodshed. The* MAHARAL
> *wipes the ax and sets it down by the*
> *woodpile.*)

MAHARAL. (*Calmly.*) What have you done?
    Do you know what you've done?
GOLEM. I've spilled blood.
MAHARAL. Do you know whose blood
    you've spilled?
GOLEM. Jewish blood.

MAHARAL. O God,
    I wanted to create a protector,
    but instead I created a monster!
    Are we being punished, O Lord,
    because we wished to protect ourselves?
    Don't you approve?
    Was he not created through you?
    Why such chastisement? Why?
    Did you permit me
    to create this man of earth,
    only to see at last
    my insignificance and my great sin?

    (*Pause.*) Is it a sin, O Lord,
    to protect yourself?
    To do what the enemy does?
    To use force, might, and violence
    and evoke terror?
    The very blood I hoped to save I've shed.
    In copying the enemy,
    I've let the enemy triumph! (*Pause.*)

    (*To heaven.*) O God,
    my tragedy is one you understand:
    My creation does not act
    in accordance with my plan!

    (*To the* GOLEM.) And you,
    why are you silent?
    You who found the ax so useful, speak!
    Let my neck bend before you
    so that you may cut off my head
    or split it in two!

GOLEM. (*Lovingly*.) Maharal.
MAHARAL. (*Reflecting*.)
    Can he even be charged with guilt?
    No. How can he? And now?
    What is to be done now?
GOLEM. You'll be with me—always.
MAHARAL. A prisoner of your ax and fist?
GOLEM. Stay with me—or I'll have to—
MAHARAL. —exert violence again
    and terrorize all? (*Pause*.)
    Did you plan this?
GOLEM. No, I didn't plan it.
    It emerged from my longing.
MAHARAL. Your longing?
    Longing to keep me all for yourself?
    Am I to sit here, sleep here, eat here, always?
GOLEM. (*Happily*.) You'll always be with me!
    Sit down, Maharal. You look tired. Rest!

> (*The* MAHARAL *sits down on the
> bench, holding his head in his
> hands. The* GOLEM *stands beside
> him, smiling and calm*.)

You won't go away, Maharal?
MAHARAL. No. I'll stay here.
    I'll not leave.
    The congregation will say the Sabbath prayers
    without me and go home.
    It will be unlike any Sabbath
    we've ever known.
    And you and I will be here together,
    just as we are now.

(EVA, *weeping, runs from the side doorway of the shul into the courtyard and bursts into the woodshed.*)

EVA. Grampa! Grampa!

GOLEM. (*Happily.*) Oh, Maharal, look!
It's Eva!

MAHARAL. (*Raising his head.*)
What is it, my child?

EVA. Grampa, everyone is weeping.
Come back to the shul!

GOLEM. Don't cry, Eva.
The Maharal is staying with me.
Have you come to stay with me, too?

EVA. (*Attacking the* GOLEM, *beating his chest with her hands.*) Murderer!

GOLEM. Oh, Eva, (*Tenderly embracing her.*)
where have you been
these past few days?
You are so good!
How sweet the smell of your hair!
How warm your hands!
You've come to me at last!
You're mine!

EVA. Monster! (*Beating the* GOLEM *again.*)

GOLEM. (*Smiling.*) No need for shouting.
No need for hitting.
The Maharal doesn't shout or hit.

EVA. Go away!

GOLEM. Why go away when I'm so happy?
You make me so happy!

MAHARAL. (*Slowly standing.*) Joseph!
      You are a golem!
      (*Contemptuously.*) A golem!

> (*The* GOLEM *shrinks as he releases*
> EVA, who *runs and throws her*
> *arms around the* MAHARAL.)

EVA. Grampa, come back to the shul.
      The congregation won't stop weeping
      and won't say the prayers without you.
MAHARAL. Tell them I'm coming.

> (EVA *runs out and enters the main*
> *doorway of the shul.*)

GOLEM. Why did she run away?
MAHARAL. Because your last mission
      is about to begin,
      and no one must witness it but me.
GOLEM. Mission? What mission?
MAHARAL. We must hurry.
GOLEM. Hurry where?
MAHARAL. We don't have too much time.
      Only a few minutes remain.
      Once the sun sets,
      and the Sabbath has begun,
      it will be too late
      to do your final task.
GOLEM. What must I do?
MAHARAL. It's easy.
      It's all been decided and sealed.
      And all is forgiven.

GOLEM. I'll obey you, Maharal.
　　Send me, and I'll go.
MAHARAL. No need to go anywhere.
　　Right here, before my eyes,
　　you'll complete your mission.
　　Now lie down on the ground.
　　The earth's growing still and beginning to rest.
　　Everything rests when the Sabbath comes,
　　and the Sabbath is about to begin.
　　You, too, will rest.
　　Just lie down on the ground.
GOLEM. (*Lying supine on the mat.*) I'm lying on
　　the ground, Maharal. (*Suddenly sitting up,
　　trembling with fear.*)
　　What will you do with me?
　　What are you going to do?
MAHARAL. (*Reassuring.*) Everything's all right.
　　Just do as I say.

　　　　(*The* GOLEM, *weeping, stretches
　　　　out his arms and tightly embraces
　　　　the* MAHARAL*'s legs.*)

GOLEM. Maharal, please,
　　I don't want to die.
　　I'm afraid to die.
　　Maharal, don't command me to lie down.
MAHARAL. Lie down.
　　Everything's all right.
　　Everything will be as it was before.
　　And you'll be happy.

(*The   GOLEM   releases   the*
MAHARAL, *lies supine, and does
not move.*)

GOLEM. I'm lying down. (*Flexing his knees.*)
MAHARAL. Extend your legs and relax.
GOLEM. (*Extending and relaxing his legs.*)
    You won't leave me, will you, Maharal?
MAHARAL. No. I'm right here beside you.
    Keep your legs stretched out.
    Now close your eyes.
GOLEM. (*Keeping legs extended, closing his
    eyes.*) My eyes are closed.
MAHARAL. (*Chanting, eyes closed, hands over
    the* GOLEM.)
    May the spirit leave this golem.
    And may God forgive me for what I've done!
    O God!
    Let this man of earth return to earth!

(*Looking   toward   heaven,   arms   upward,
incanting.*)

    EH-met! EH-met! EH-met!
    Truth! Truth! Truth!

(*Turning toward the* GOLEM, *arms spread
over him, continuing the incantation.*)

    Met! Met! Met!
    Death! Death! Death!

(*The* GOLEM *suddenly arches his back in spasm, takes one audible breath, slowly relaxes, then expires.*)

(*Reciting* Genesis 3:19.)
"You return to the ground,
for out of it you were taken;
you are dust,
and to dust you shall return."

(*Facing heaven, weeping, sobbing.*)
O God!
Forgive me!
Help me find the way!
There has to be a way!

(*For a moment, the* MAHARAL *stares at the dead GOLEM. Then with head erect, he walks resolutely from the woodshed towards the main doorway of the shul.*)

MAHARAL. (*At the main doorway, raising his arms over the congregation.*)
Everyone!
The Sabbath has just begun!
Let us give praise to the Lord!

(*Slow fade-out.*)

THE END

THE PLAYWRIGHT

Howard Rubenstein is a physician and a playwright. He was born in 1931 in Chicago and received a B.A. from Carleton College in 1953 and an M.D. from Harvard Medical School in 1957. In 1967 he was appointed Physician and Chief of Allergy at the Harvard University Health Services, a position he held until 1989, when he became a medical consultant to the Department of Social Services, State of California, a position he held until 2000, the year he retired from the practice of medicine.

Rubenstein translated Aeschylus' *Agamemnon*, which was produced at Granite Hills Acting Workshop (GHAW), El Cajon, California, in 1997. A videotape of a performance of that production was requested by Oliver Taplin, Regius Professor, Oxford, and may be found in the Archive of Performances of Greek and Roman Drama, University of Oxford, England. Rubenstein then translated and adapted Euripides' *The Trojan Women*, produced at GHAW in 2001. That production was the most decorated show, professional and amateur, of the 2001 San Diego theater season (*San Diego Playbill*). *Brothers All*, a play based on Dostoyevsky's *The Brothers Karamazov*, had its premiere at 6th@Penn Theatre in San Diego in 2006. Rubenstein has also written *Maccabee*, an epic in free verse, and co-authored with his wife, Judith S. Rubenstein, *Becoming Free*, a haggadah for Passover, and *Songs of the Seder*, a music book to accompany any haggadah.